The International Design Library

THE SCIENCE FICTION DESIGN COLORING BOOK

Brad Hamann

Stemmer House
PUBLISHERS, INC.
OWINGS MILLS, MARYLAND

INTRODUCTION

Disclaimer from the Board of Trustees — The University of Callisto

"The members of the board wish to officially disassociate themselves and the university from Professor Phillip Starlowe and his work. He was sent to Zantee with certain tasks of a professional and scholarly nature to perform. These he did complete. But Professor Starlowe also chose to take on other tasks of a completely different nature, thus overstepping set bounds, challenging the existing parameters of his assignment, and questioning the authority of the military personnel in charge of the exploratory mission. For this blatant compromising of his position at the university we find no other option than to condemn his actions and officially withdraw support from the publication of these notes and drawings."

Excerpts from Phillip Starlowe's Journal

—It was not the things so different that impressed me, but the things so very much the same that touched me.

—In Zantee there was an inherent majesty, a naive kind of beauty such as one perceives when gazing into the unblinking eyes of a child.

—The people of Zantee had so very much to teach us in the ways of compassion, nobility of spirit, and generosity. But nobody back on earth was listening. That is why I went back to Zantee to stay.

—The mission I arrived with was of a basically military nature. There was only one question to be asked: Could Zantee be of any military use as either an outpost or base? When Zantee's desolation led to a negative answer, the military lost all interest and withdrew, without realizing the wealth of culture they had overlooked.

Fragment from the "Hislan History of the Planet Zantee" by Maal

—Our planet danced slowly about its two suns with the grace of an equillor just grown to maturity. Even though the Hislans travelled the galaxies at will, we felt at home only on humble Zantee.

—We had been witness to spectacular events as we roamed freely through the cosmos, yet it was the sight of Zantee growing larger in the view ports of our returning ships that quickened the pulse and stirred the soul.

—And now I look about me and see only destruction. My home is no more. This horror fell upon us so quickly that the few of us left alive can put no name to those who brought our world to an end. But we will discover that name some day, and it will live forever as a curse upon the lips of my people.

Description of the Plates

Plate 1 Title Page This is a reproduction of a mural which decorates the outside wall of the library at the university. It was painted by Daniel Routh III, a descendant of a twentieth-century artist. It depicts Horace the God of Robotics drawing forth from the air the components from which he will build the first free-thinking biots. Daniel is a good friend of mine and was commissioned by the board of trustees to paint several murals, a few of which I have reproduced here in my notes. The actual size is 50 meters by 38 meters.

Plate 2 Zantee is a planet in a binary star system. The two suns move quickly across the sky together although the smaller and farther, Ro, sets slower as it nears the horizon and rules the twilight hours after Rila has set. Depicted here is an Equillor, the small swift plains animal which travels in herds across the flatlands near the equator.

Plate 3 Our encampment was erected at the perimeter of a vast and terribly desolate plain that Xanor referred to as the Field of Tears. Apparently it was the site where the last handful of Zantee warriors died defending the sanctity of their home planet. Some cruel outpouring of energy had fused the battlefield into a silvery glassine surface. Often, after I had finished cataloging the day's finds, I would sit at the edge of this plain lost in thought as I watched the constellations revolve slowly overhead. One evening while the rest of the camp slept, I arose from a restless sleep and crept down the embankment to the shore of this solid sea. Suddenly, there appeared before me, without a sound, a dozen pairs of gracefully floating shapes I can only describe as serpentine in form. Each looped shape approached its companion, arching and writhing in what appeared to be a ritual courtship dance which lasted for over an hour. As they joined themselves together, I was filled with a deep pity and sadness. And as I watched, they slowly drifted earthward and disappeared into apertures which silently opened in the surface below and just as silently closed, leaving no mark or trace to show they had ever been.

I awoke the next morning and told Xanor of my vision, which seemed dreamlike in the morning sun. Laconic as always, Xanor would only say that according to legends, on certain nights the life forces of the Zantee warriors would grow restless, and yearning to see again the night sky, would rise from their amber-like prisons to dance below the stars they loved so dearly. Xanor spoke softly and when he had finished, he turned slowly from me and went back to gathering herbs for my lists. He never spoke of the Plain again and I asked no more of him regarding it.

Plates 4, 5   Xanor led me through the dusty streets and shattered ruins of his village one afternoon, saying little as usual. He took me up a flight of dark and broken stone steps and I was introduced to Xola, the eldest of Xanor's people and chief archivist of Zantee. Among the materials he showed me was a tapestry of two combatants riding Branks and wearing the ceremonial armor of the Hislans, the guardian warriors of Zantee. The joust shown here was part of an annual competition which took place each fall to celebrate the end of the harvest season. The last fall fair took place nearly 5,000 years ago, before the Zantee civilization was brought to its knees by the lightening strike of an unknown horde from an equally unknown part of the universe. I questioned Xola about the identity of this army but he claimed that the few survivors had never discovered the identity of the mysterious race which blasted Zanteen culture back to the equivalent of the stone age.

Plates 6, 7   Zantee craftspeople took great pride in producing armor and weaponry which combined beauty, function, and the ability to strike fear into the heart of an adversary. These samples are shown at approximately one-third of their actual size. Xola felt it was important that I realize that the design of these pieces was meant to deter any actual violence; to discourage the outbreak of battle from the start. This seems to have been a successful premise, for in over 50,000 years of recorded Zanteen history, less than a score of alien fatalities have been noted. It is an advanced race indeed that takes pride in the lack of blood spilt in its name.

Plates 8, 9   Ceremonial shields and swords. The left shield depicts Loo-Rong the Batrachian, a deity said to inhabit the mist-covered swamps of the Green Region. Displayed at right is a shield bearing the image of Il-Kanon, guardian of the marshlands of the Turquoise Lowlands.

Plates 10, 11   The Tobias Grace Memorial Mask Collection.

About a month after my arrival on Zantee I was doing some minor digging among the ruins at the outskirts of Matee I, a small fishing community, when I unearthed what appeared to be a beautifully stylized mask fashioned out of Olnex, a Zanteen alloy. Inlaid with multi-colored and highly reflective enamels, the white metal blazed in the afternoon sun as I brushed the reddish soil from its surface. Xanor became greatly agitated (for him) and excitedly explained that this was one of the Eight Players. These, he explained, comprised a group of masks created for a traveling morality play which swept across the planet in Brankor-drawn wagons. Xanor suspected that the rest of the set was buried further down in the soil. I had found the first at a depth of a dozen krons, or roughly five meters. I had not the funds to hire the local workers I would need to do a more extensive dig, so returning quickly to our camp I sent a plea for funds back to the University. I waited two days for a reply. The University was not able to extend me additional credit at this time, but an alumna, Matilda Grace, had heard of my plight and ordered her credit account put at my disposal. She asked only that the collection of masks, if found to be complete, be dedicated in memory of her great-great-grandfather, Tobias Grace, a 20th-century traveling showman and puppeteer. I transmitted my joyful thanks and, hiring the workers, was able to uncover the complete set of eight masks. Xola was able to supply me with the following background on each mask:

Plate 10   The Wind Carrier—represented the indiscriminate forces of nature. He knows not the difference between good and evil, and is a very important variable in the evolution of any intelligent race.

Plate 11   The Equillor—the representative of the Zanteen animal kingdom, who, although incapable of speech, commands a great voice in the planet's destiny.

Plate 12   At one time, as recently as 50,000 years ago, Zantee had been a planet with a vast network of natural waterways. These spiderwebbed the northern hemisphere at a great distance from the arid desert areas at the equator. The small seas which formed at the conjunctions of the larger rivers of the north were populated by the Garoondi, a peaceful and quite intelligent species whose exoskeletons served both a protective and an aesthetic role. Leatherish to the touch, the bony outer covering was articulated by bristling waves of movement set off by the intricately controlled undulations of the underlying muscles. The Garoondi used vibratory patterns to compose epic poems in celebration of the boundless joy and freedom they felt as they swam great distances through the aqua-colored waters. But eventually the Garoondi disappeared, not unlike their poems, among the waves which broke upon the beaches of the coastline. Their fate remains a mystery, and the universe is a poorer place for their leaving.

Plate 13   The most vicious of Zantee's life forms, the Pterozons dwelt among the cliffs at the edge of the deserts in the south. Their cruising range was vast, over 5,000 kilokrons. They would often sweep over the northern seas and attack the Garoondi. Sometimes an overconfident pterozon would fly for too long a time over the surface of the water and find himself dragged under by several Garoondi. A balance of a sort was thus achieved.

Plate 14   This is another Routh mural from the University. As Dan explained it: "To a terran, this creature personifies that which repulses, which fills one with utter loathing and causes one to turn away. But in actuality this creature, whose name is Fron, is a very skilled surgeon from the fog-planet Sorelle. He is the embodiment of compassion and generosity. He has traveled from star system to star system, answering the distant calls of those in need. He has served in 417 different interplanetary conflicts, lessening the pain and anguish of those on either side of the battle. I spoke with him briefly when I was assigned to cover the Claunion Conflict as a sketch artist. His reputation had preceded him and I asked him why he devoted his entire existence to this unending mission. He looked up from his work on a young Claunion foot soldier and turned his dark amber eyes towards the front line 500 krons off, listening to the distant clash of arms and the cries of the wounded. "There is no mission," he whispered, still gazing into the distance. "There is no purpose. No reason. There is no pain, and no merit is sought or acquired."

Plate 15 Xanor showed me a small icon, a painting depicting Grellia and Sando, the wife and child of the mightiest of the Hislans, Maal. As legend has it, at one time a neighboring planet was threatened by famine and began to raid Zanteen trade ships to supply themselves with grain and spice. As the cause of these raids became apparent, Maal spoke with the high council and arranged for 1200 barges of grain to be shipped to the starving planet. He himself led the mercy mission, commandeering the Hislan flagship. But because of a communication slip-up the fleet was thought to be attacking, and a thermonuclear warhead was launched. To protect the fleet, Maal entered a shuttle and sped ahead of the Zantee barges. He took the warhead straight on, sacrificing himself. The mistake was immediately discovered and in true Zantee fashion their grain was delivered despite the incident. The Hislans returned silently homeward, ignoring the pleas of forgiveness from the aggrieved planet.

On the Hislans return, Grellia stood at the landing field waiting to welcome Maal home, with Sando in her arms. But he never arrived. She returned each night for 57 years, awaiting Maal's return, until she passed away. Sando grew to be a mighty Hislan himself and vowed never to leave Zantee again.

Plate 16 Part of the official entertainment aboard the flight which took us to Zantee.

Plate 17 A page from a Hislan training manual showing a fleet of Zantee cruisers in proper parade formation. The ships were never armed, but could reach a speed of 800 kilokrons per hour.

Plate 18 The Darkling—embodies the evil side of man's nature. He is a possessor of an insatiable appetite for war and destruction.

Plate 19 The Krull—symbolizes the rational, meditative aspect of the Zantee mind.

Centerspread The military found this deserted air strip on Zantee. Unlike the more simplistic native architecture it had a coldness about it. A feeling of menace lay about the place. Xanor told me later it was built ages ago by the invaders who had sacked Zantee. Fortunately it was well constructed and accommodated our Terran ships and camp arrangements easily. Perhaps too easily. I was nagged by suspicions even at that early point.

Plate 20 Dan Routh III chose as the subject of one of his murals the great Terran scientist Sir Stephen of Edgewick. He built and independently financed the famed Pan Galaxia, a starship equipped for scientific observation. He managed to forge the first link between Terra and an alien race, the Picanoids, in the cosmic year 1227.

Plate 21 The Trenlok was a predatory flying creature which hunted in the shallow bays near the coastlines of the north. It was characterized by its swiftness, its keen eyesight, its razorsharp talons and wingtips, and most of all by its piercing cry which it emitted whenever it successfully snatched its dinner from the saline waters.

Plates 22, 23 Tronex is a member of a marauding band of pirates whose home planet shares Zantee's suns, Ro and Rila. He commandeered a stripped-down reconnaissance cruiser equipped with a pair of Pranoline T7LS plasma thrusters he had hijacked from a Terran exploratory vessel. He was captured after a long chase when he attempted to execute a side-step into a black hole and misjudged his acceleration speed. He was trapped on the black hole's event horizon and the image of his ship will flicker spectrally on the perimeter of the anomaly for the rest of the time.

Plate 24 The Ting is a winged insectoid capable of traveling up to 25 kilokrons per hour. The Ting devours 20 times its weight in plant matter each day to maintain its weight. The Ting shown here (actual size) is about to make a meal of a Pilla plant, whose blossom exudes a thick, scented sap which the Ting saves for last.

Plate 25 The Legend of the Soft Moon.

One of the tales oft told young Zantians is that of "The Soft Moon." On a far away planet, an ancient civilization had flourished, which in its self-centered way believed that the natural state of the planet's crust was what they saw before them. To them the steel, glass, and concrete which covered every square mile of the planet had simply always been. But at last, a strange bloated form was captured by the planet's gravity, a soft, brown-green mass of organic matter. The moon drew closer and closer and the soft matter was attracted by the planet's gravitational pull and flowed down in the form of a thick protuberance. Finally the entire surface was buried under this organic mass and nothing remained of the steel, glass and concrete. The people wept for their loss, surrounded as they were by trees and plants and fields. They spent the rest of their lives trying to reconstruct the "natural state" of things—by destroying the forests, stripping the hills, and polluting the oceans. And they eventually managed to do it. "The poor fools," as grandfather would add.

Plates 26, 27   Zantee's seas were rich in life forms, ranging from the tiny ocean sparrow to the monstrous Blook. The creatures pictured here are all extinct, victims of the bombs of the unknown invaders that caused most of Zantee's water to boil off into the atmosphere.

Plate 28   This is a holosection of one of the many temporary space-hives that were constructed by the refugees from Zantee. Forced to leave the planet's surface, they wandered about the Corillian Asteroid belt and transformed the largest asteroids into livable quarters by ingeniously cannibalizing their own spacecraft. Ventilation and artificial gravity systems were devised and several generations of Zantians grew up in these hives before the planet cooled down and became safe to return to.

Plate 29   Related to the Ting (Plate 24), the Mildroc is a sightless insect which travels by thermal-radar. Supersensitive to the temperature of various foods, terrain, and its enemies, the Mildroc is literally impossible to capture. I was unable to obtain a specimen for study.

Plate 30   The Zang—the spark, the catalyst, the igniter, of man's passions and dreams.

Plate 31   The Queel—the indifference of the universe and all it encompasses, towards the insignificant employments of man.

Plates 32, 33   Two pages from a Zanteen illuminated manuscript depicting the Armagrill, the mythological beast who, when time ends, will sweep across the universe swallowing the stars until there is only darkness, and then devour itself from the tail up, leaving nothing.

Plates 34, 35   Jewelry from the collection of the Lady Marcileena. Wife of a 27th century nobleman, Lady Marcileena traveled extensively through the Scorpion Nebula as Zantee's ambassador-at-large. The two large pieces are earrings from the Teraccian spice planet. The two rings are from the Stampellian system.

Plate 36   Monument erected to the memory of Maal, greatest of the Zantee Hislans (see Plate 15).

Plate 37   A Yazz riding a Delpa. The Yazz were a highly intelligent species of water-breathers who inhabited the swamps of the Green Region. In dry seasons when it was necessary to migrate over the surrounding dry regions, the Yazz would lure Delpas into the swamps with Albex, a synthetic spice. The small-brained Delpas would be strapped into aqua-harnesses which included an Albex feedbag. The Yazz thus made their way across the desert areas riding the addicted Delpas.

Plate 38   The idiot—symbolizes the blind masses who follow without thinking and without inquiry.

Plate 39   The Mithrillian—represents the bitter humor, the cosmic giggle which underlies the self-important panderings of man.

Plate 40   A page from a child's nursery school primer depicting the Jade Mylando. This beetle had a mating cycle of 100 terran years. Once in a century the male would collect a Yulan Berry, and carefully drill a series of openings in it. The berry was presented to the female who either crushed the berry, thus rejecting the male, or discarded the berry and ran headlong into the male's waiting arms. The primer points out the extreme caution of the female Mylando, which resulted in many disappointed suitors and few discarded berries. Because of its extreme rarity, a drilled Yulan berry in hand will buy a vast estate on Zantee. Depicted with the Jade Mylando is a sample of Zantian jewelry-making. A crescent-shaped neck pendant is shown with an inset Yulan berry. The designs are cloisonné enamel in a background of local alloy.

Plate 41   The dance of Zeeva.
   Xola spoke reverentially as he showed me this hand-painted panel. Zeeva, he told me, was the greatest of the Zanteen deities. The Zantians believe that the universe undergoes an infinite number of deaths and rebirths and is, in actuality, only the dream of Zeeva, who, after a hundred billion years, dissolves himself into a dreamless sleep. The universe dissolves along with him until eons later, when Zeeva stirs, recomposes himself and begins to dream the great cosmic dream.
   Zeeva has four hands. In the upper left hand is a thruster engine, whose blast is the sound of creation. In the upper right hand is a tongue of nuclear flame, a reminder that the universe, now newly created, will billions of years from now be utterly destroyed.

Plate 42   Xanor posed reluctantly for this holosection which I took not long before I left Zantee. If he appears a bit grumpy it is because he was fighting a mild form of flu and had not slept well for at least a week. I must admit I was initially repulsed by his appearance, but I grew to respect and admire him during the months he aided me in my work. He is shown here proudly holding the battle helmet once owned by his grandfather Xendol. It was his only possession of value and he used it as a pillow when he slept. With my help, he was able to calculate his approximate age which was about 750 terran years, still a young man by his race's standards. I often watched him as he worked with his plants and herbs and he had a gentleness about him which taught me much. He spoke little, observed a great deal and shared his silent love of Zantee with me. In the end it was perhaps Xanor's friendship that helped me to make the final decision to return to Zantee to live permanently.

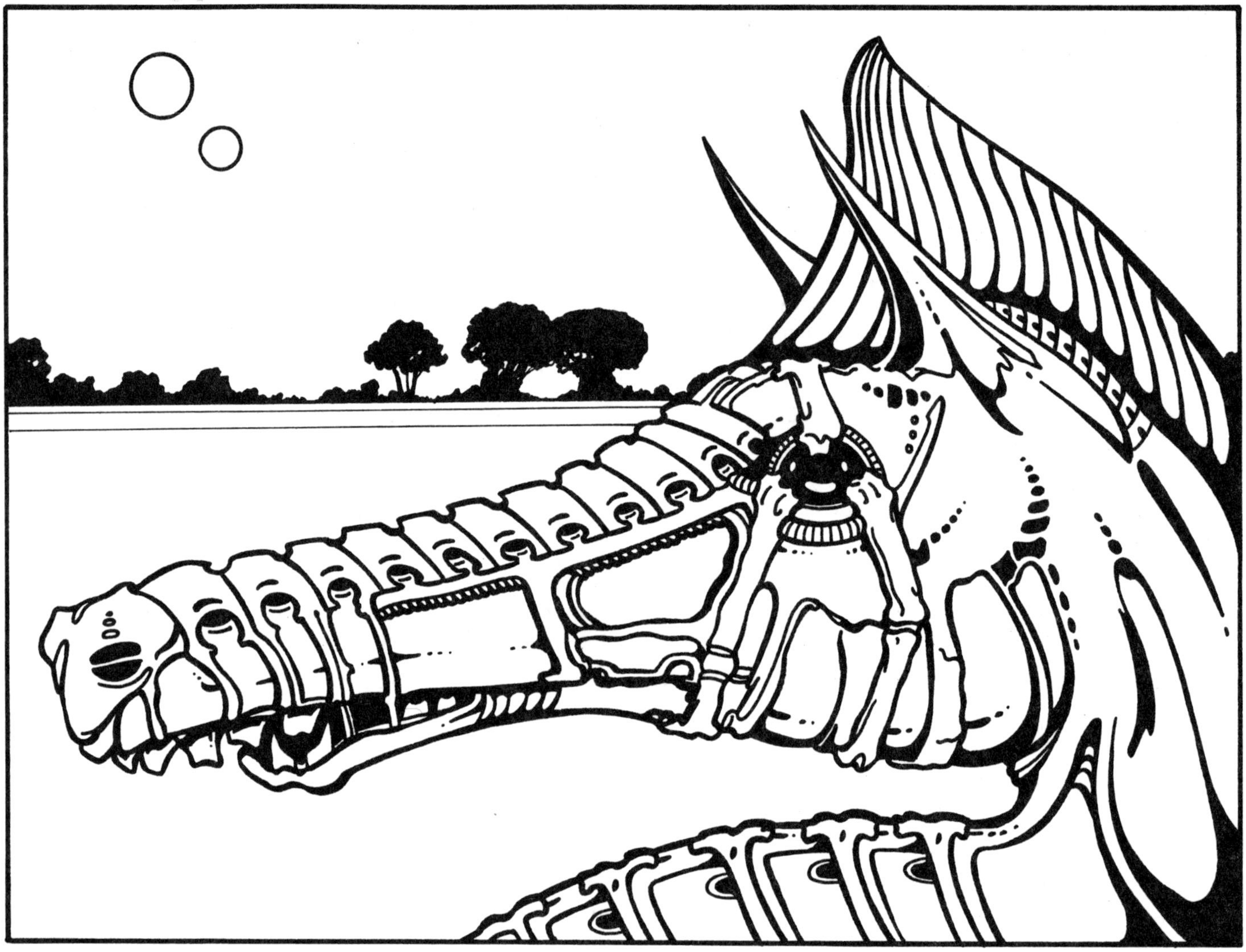

Plate 2

Plates 4, 5

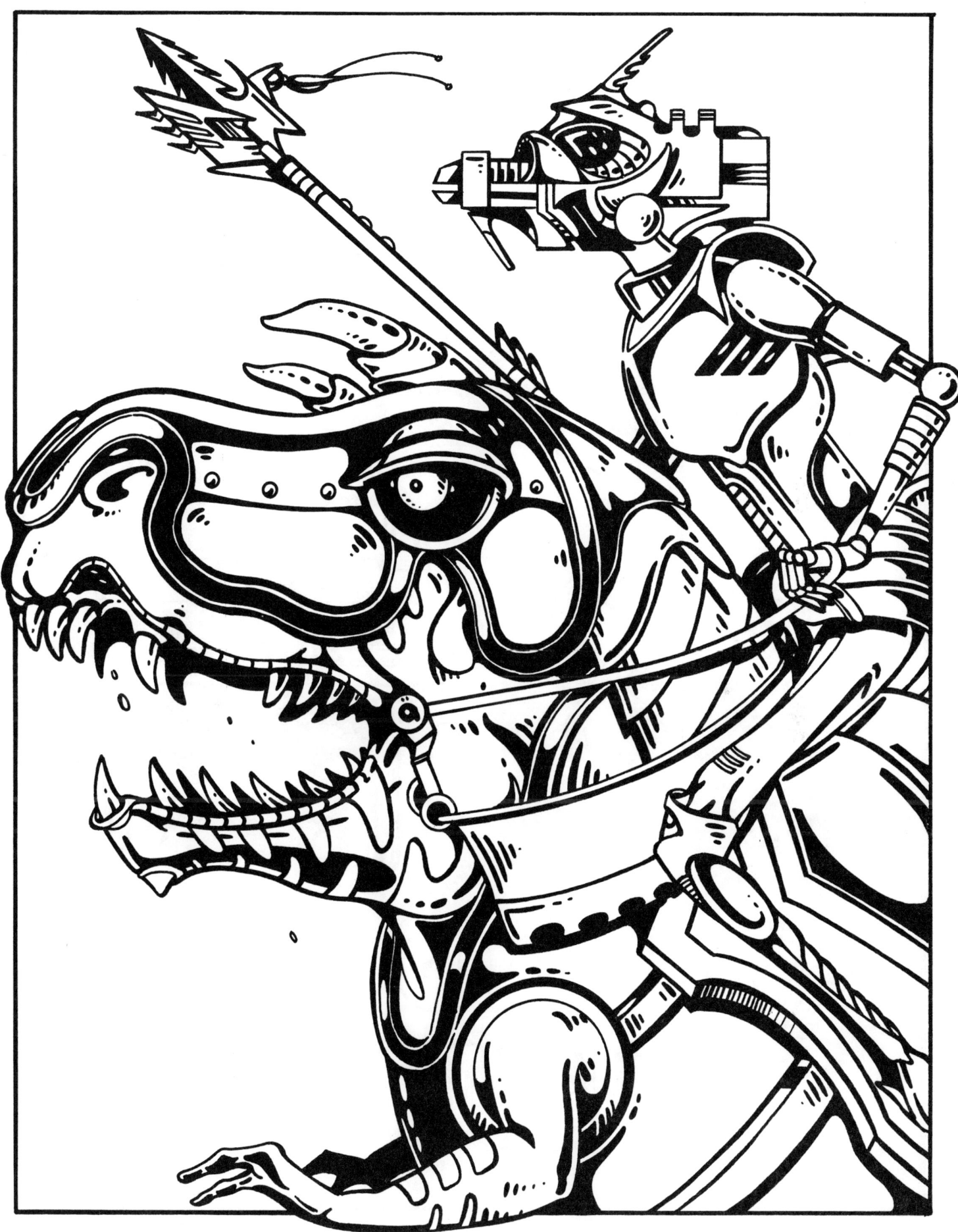

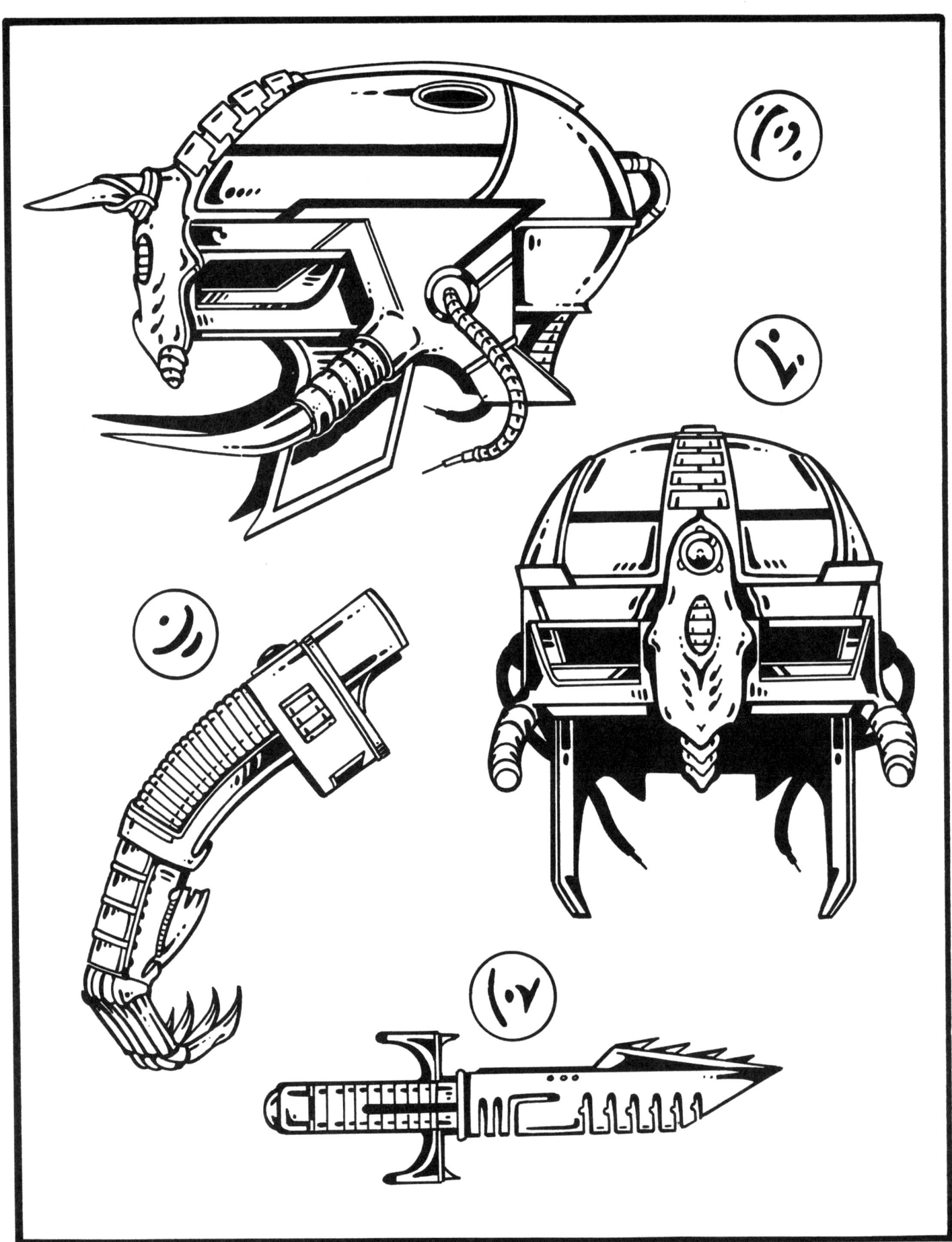

Plates 8, 9

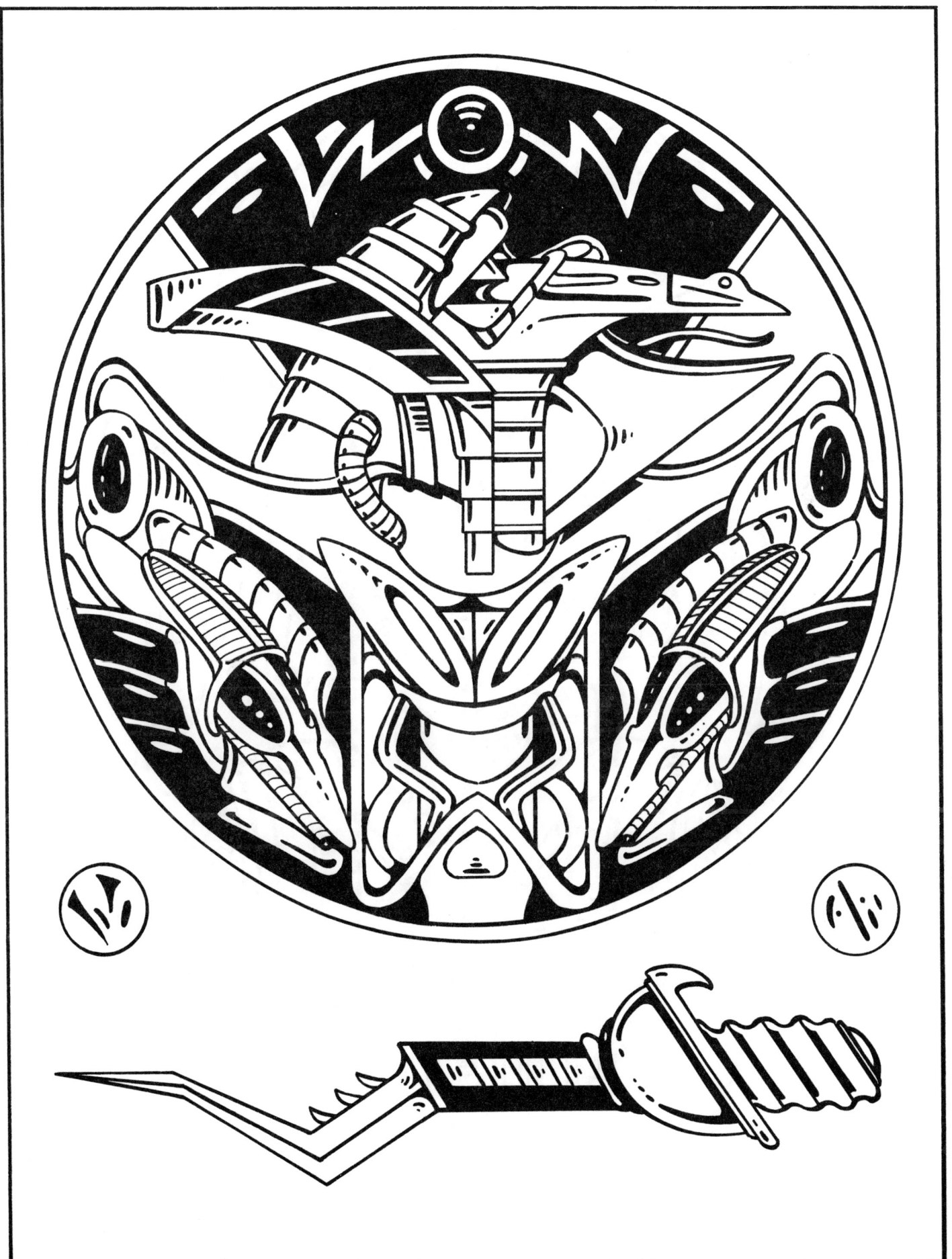

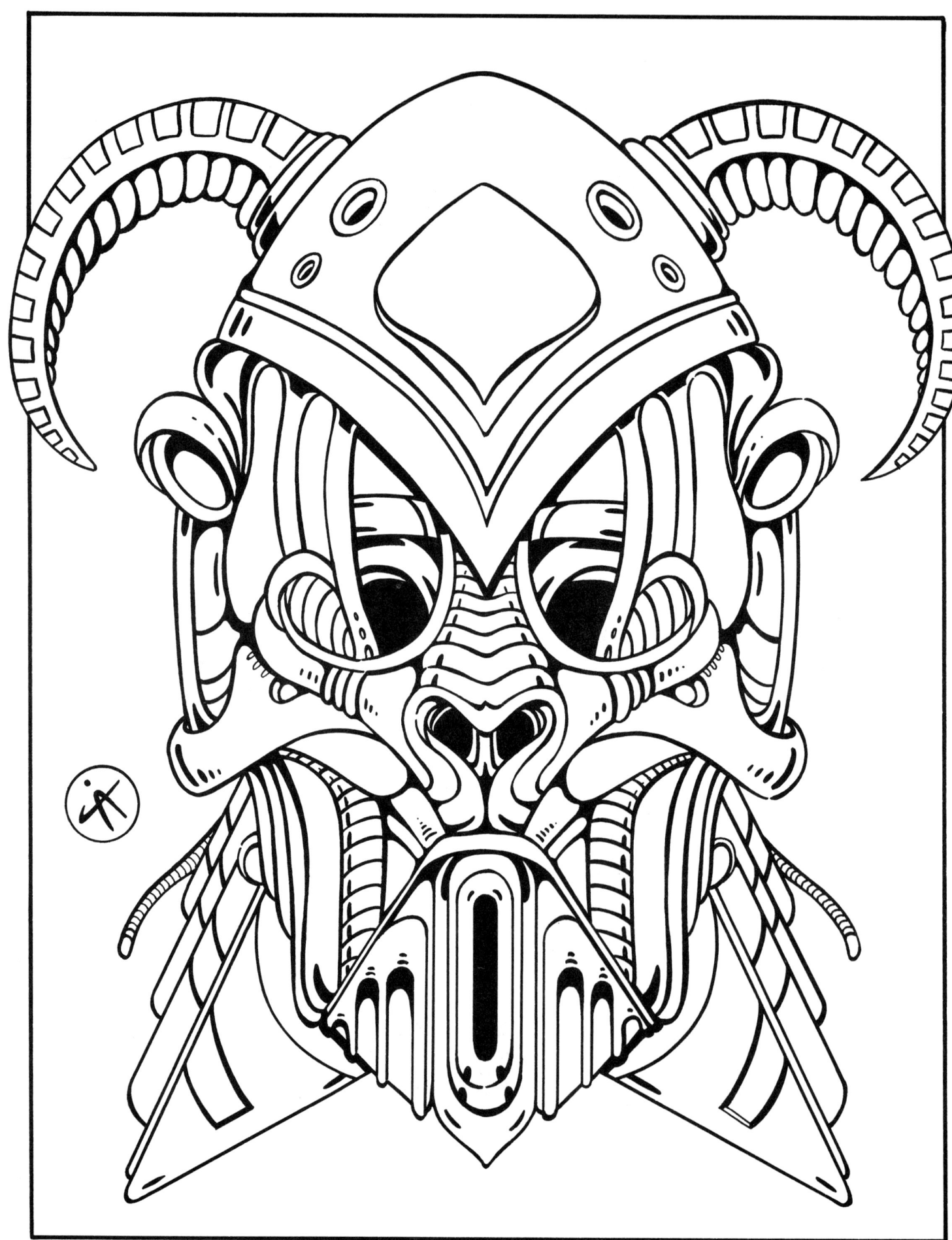

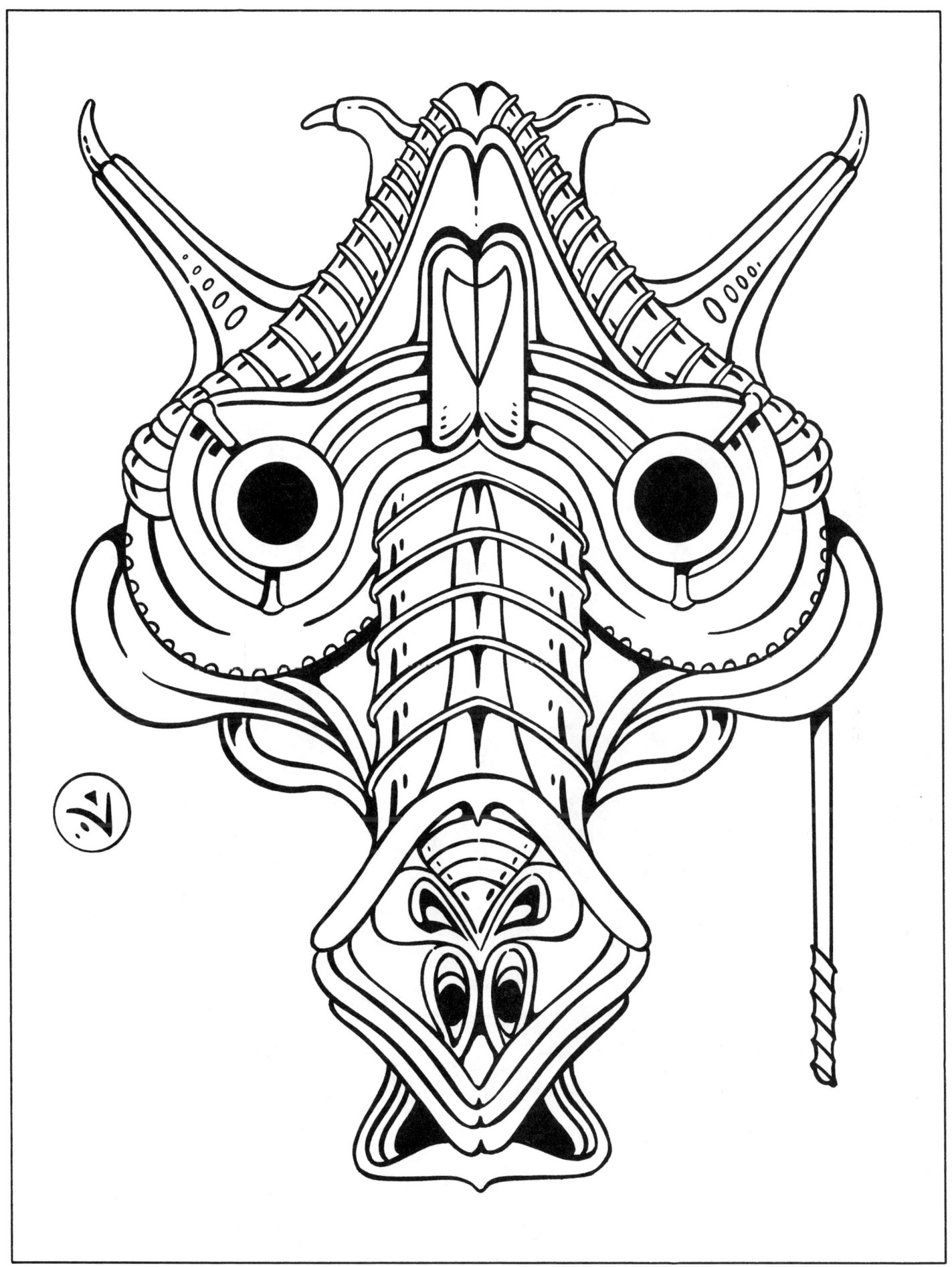

Plate 12

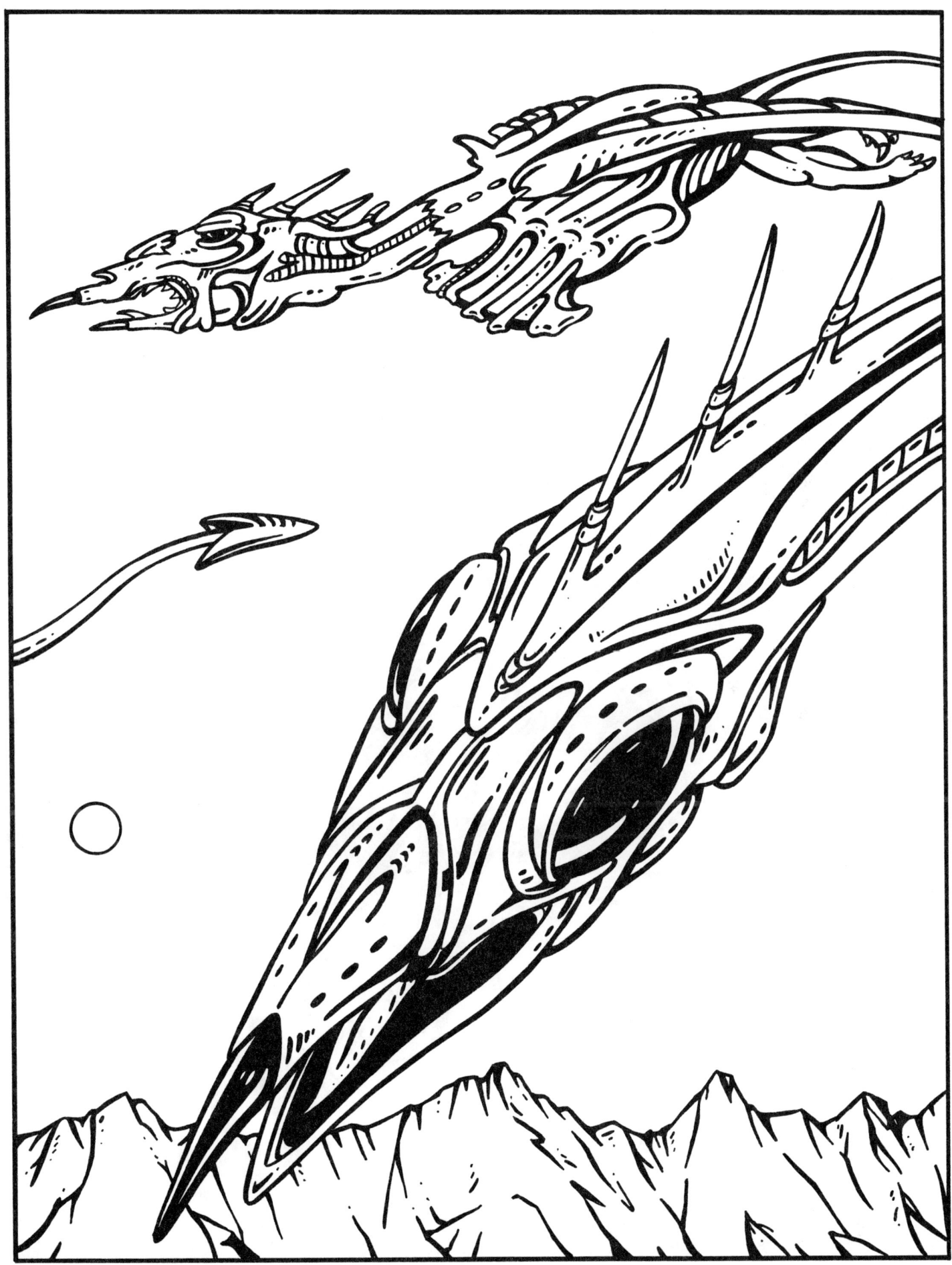

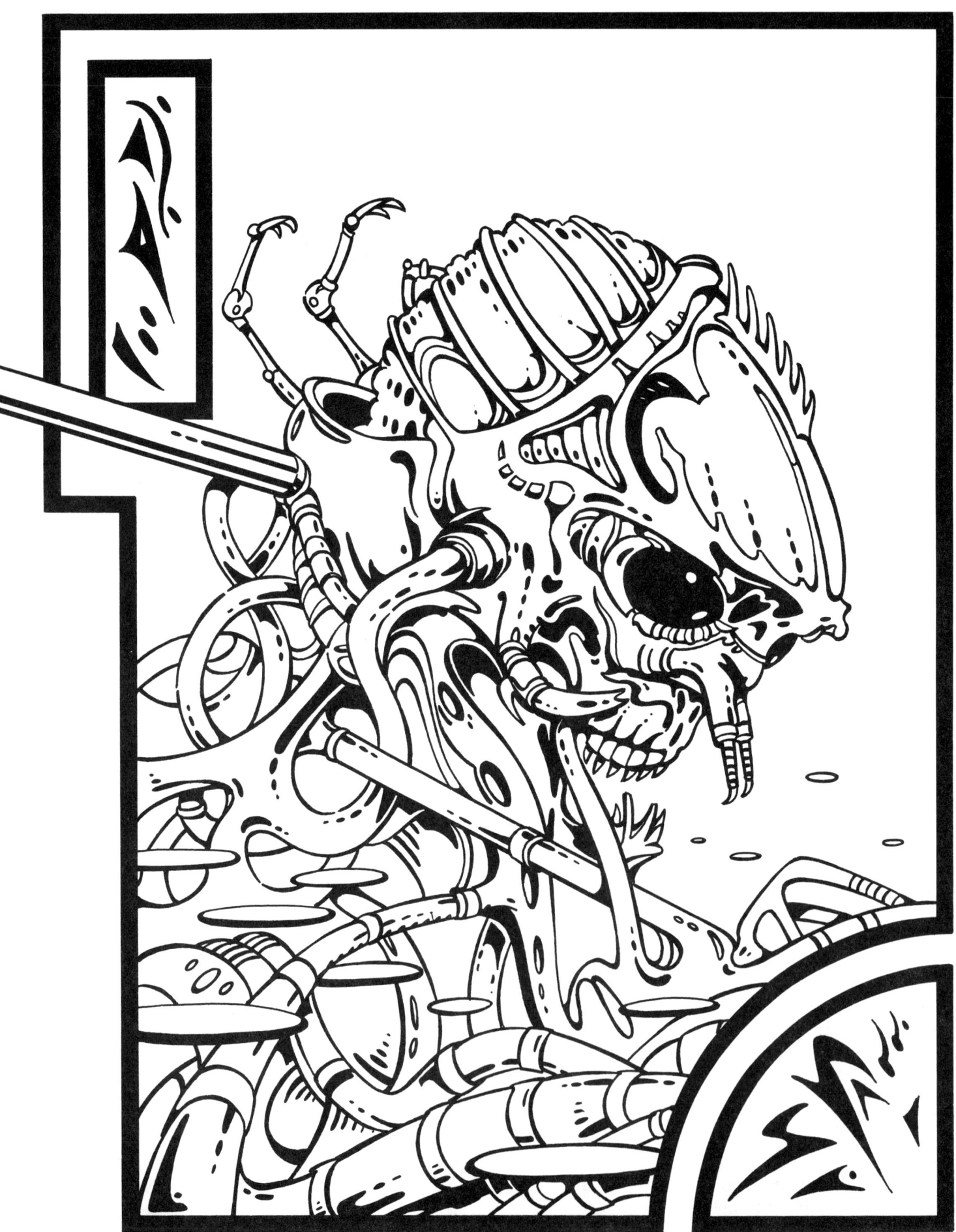

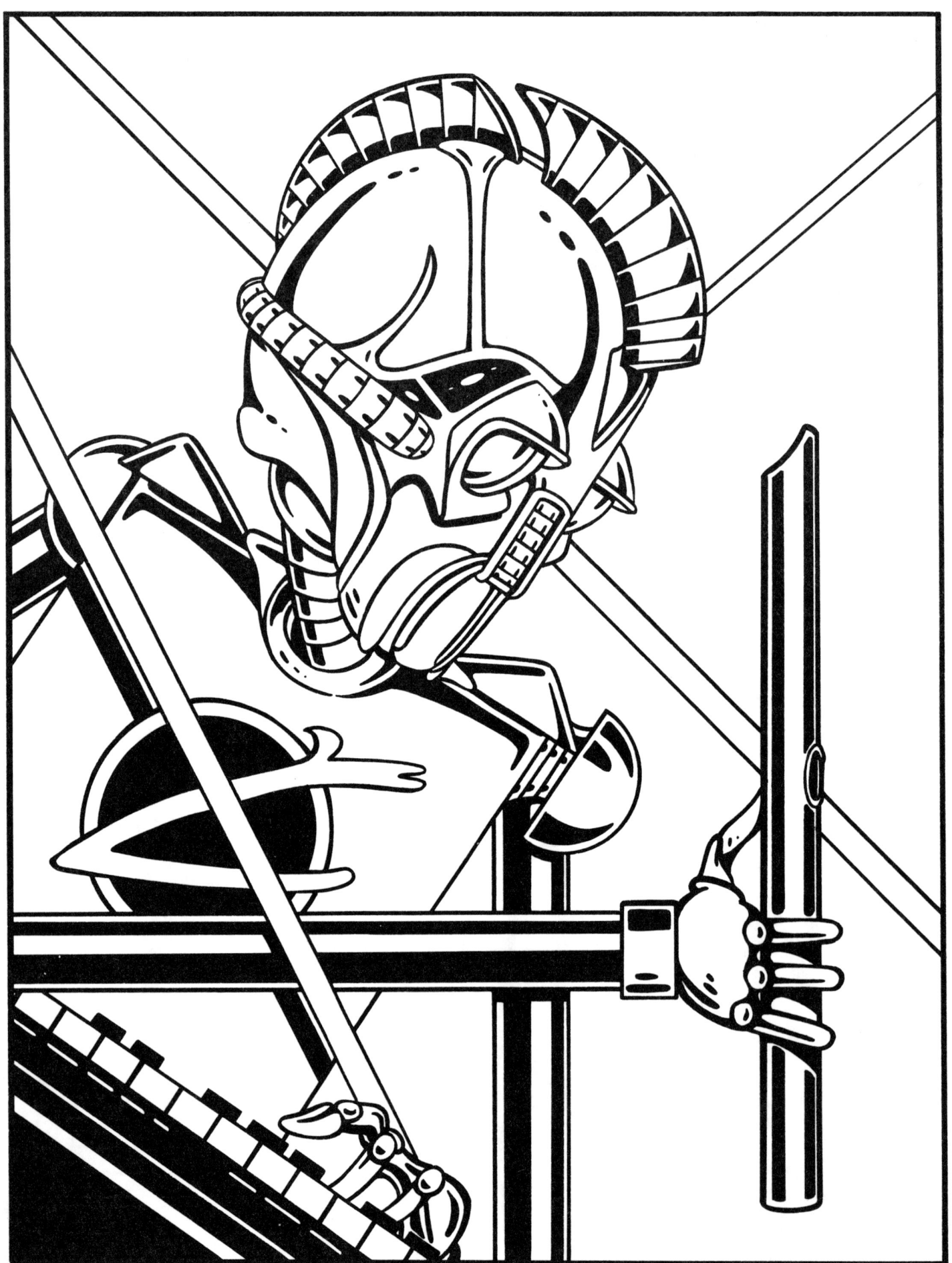

Centerspread

Plate 20

Plate 21

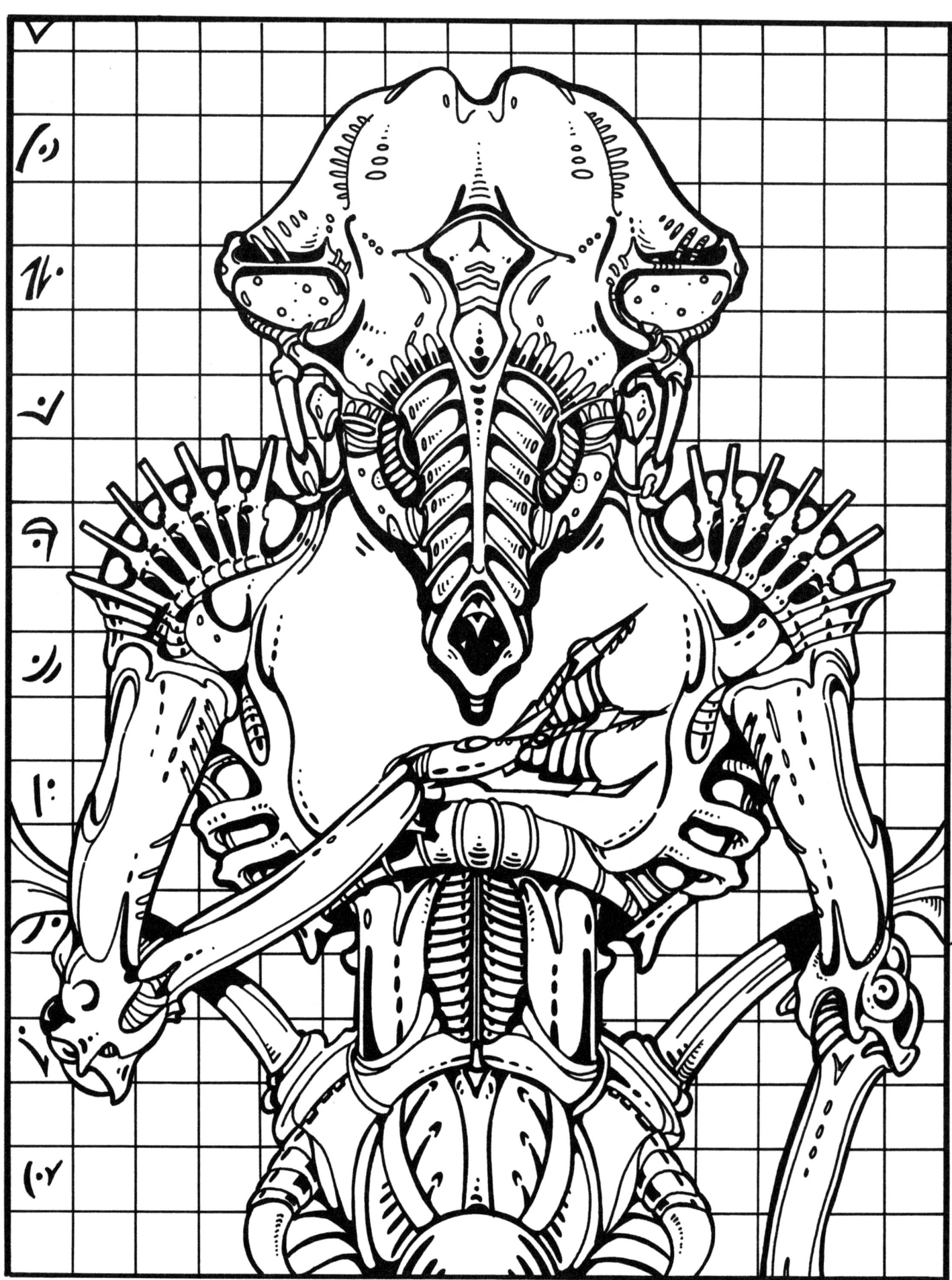

Plates 22, 23

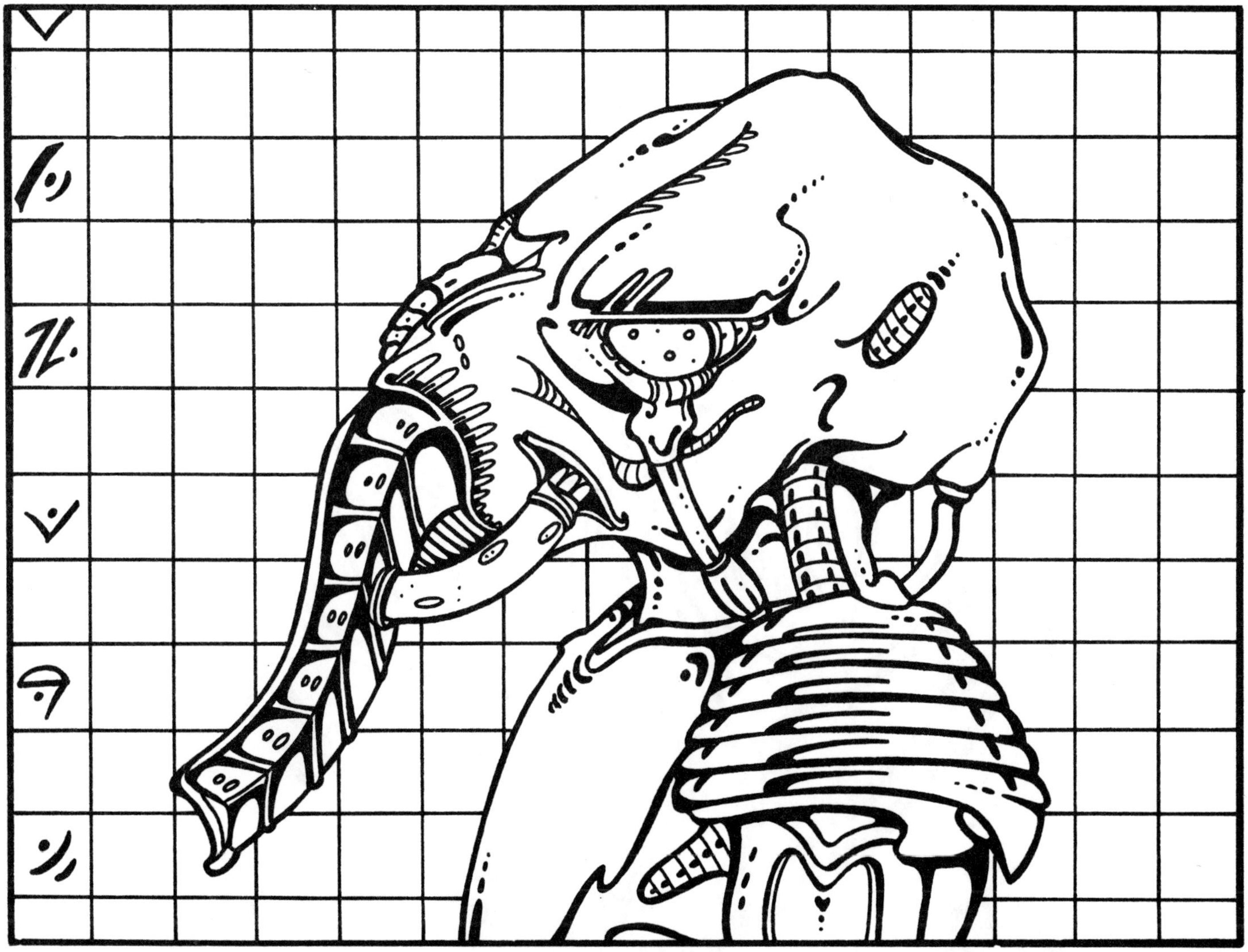

Plates 26, 27

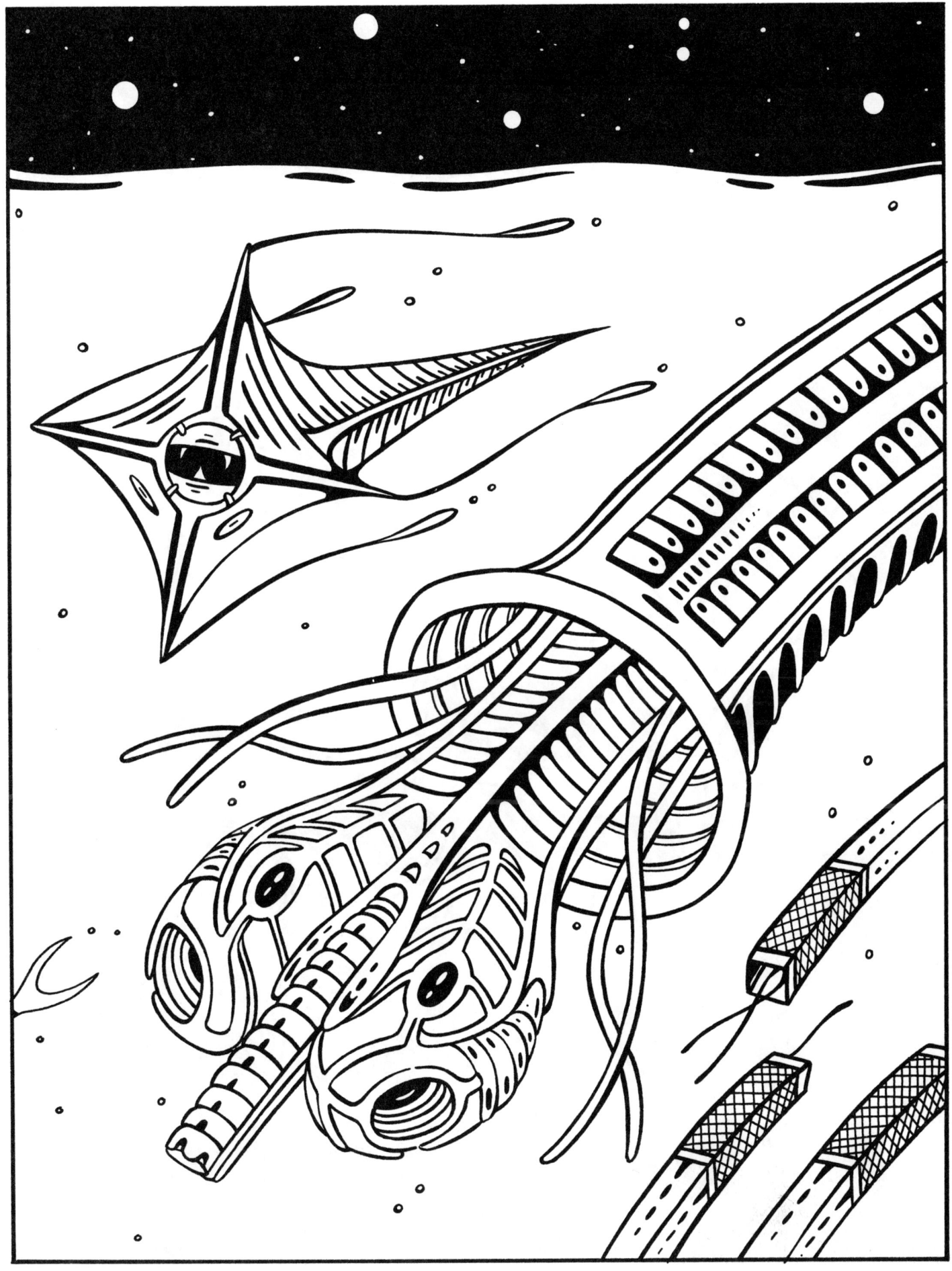

Plate 28

Plate 29

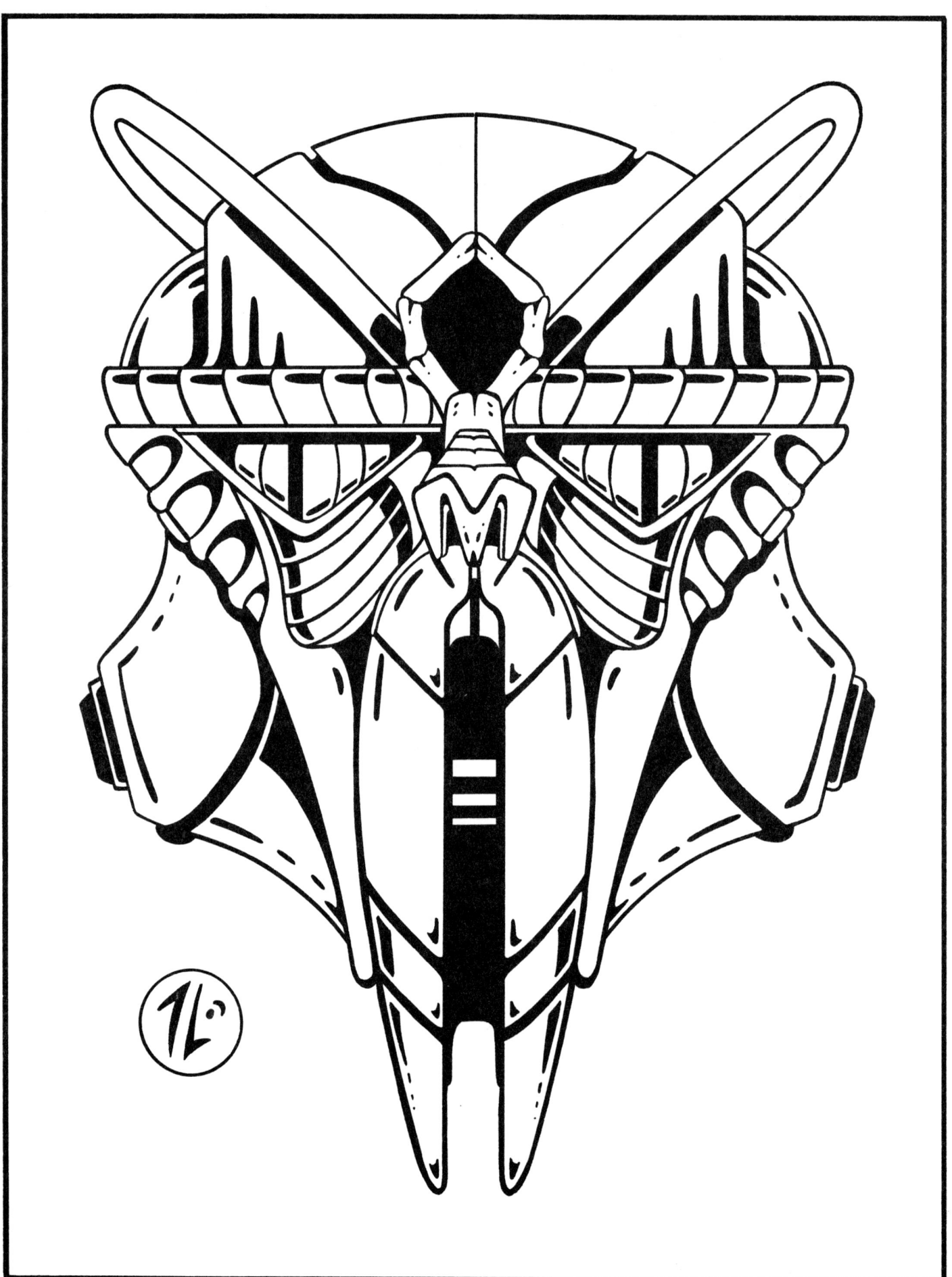

Plates 32, 33

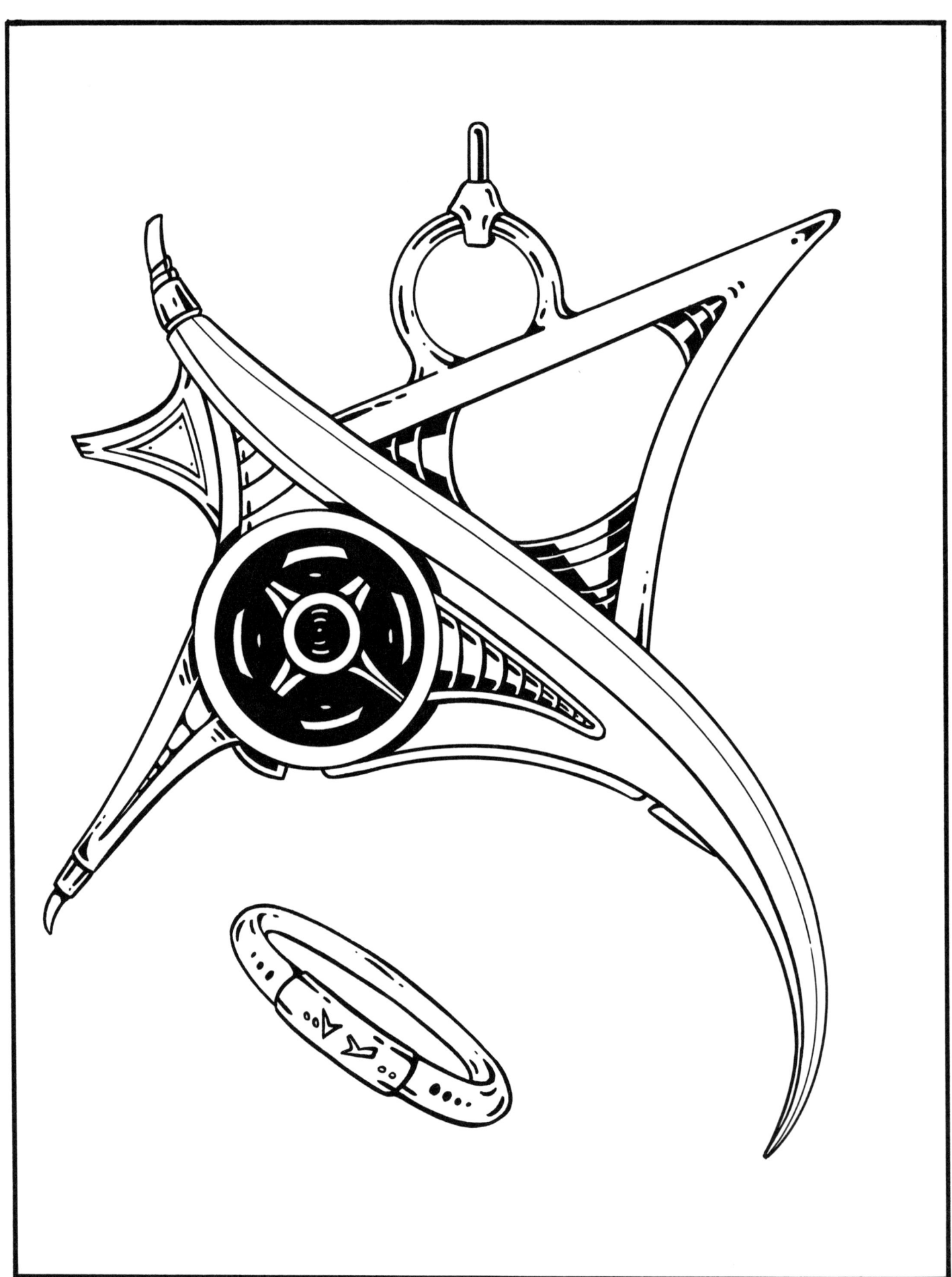

Plates 34, 35

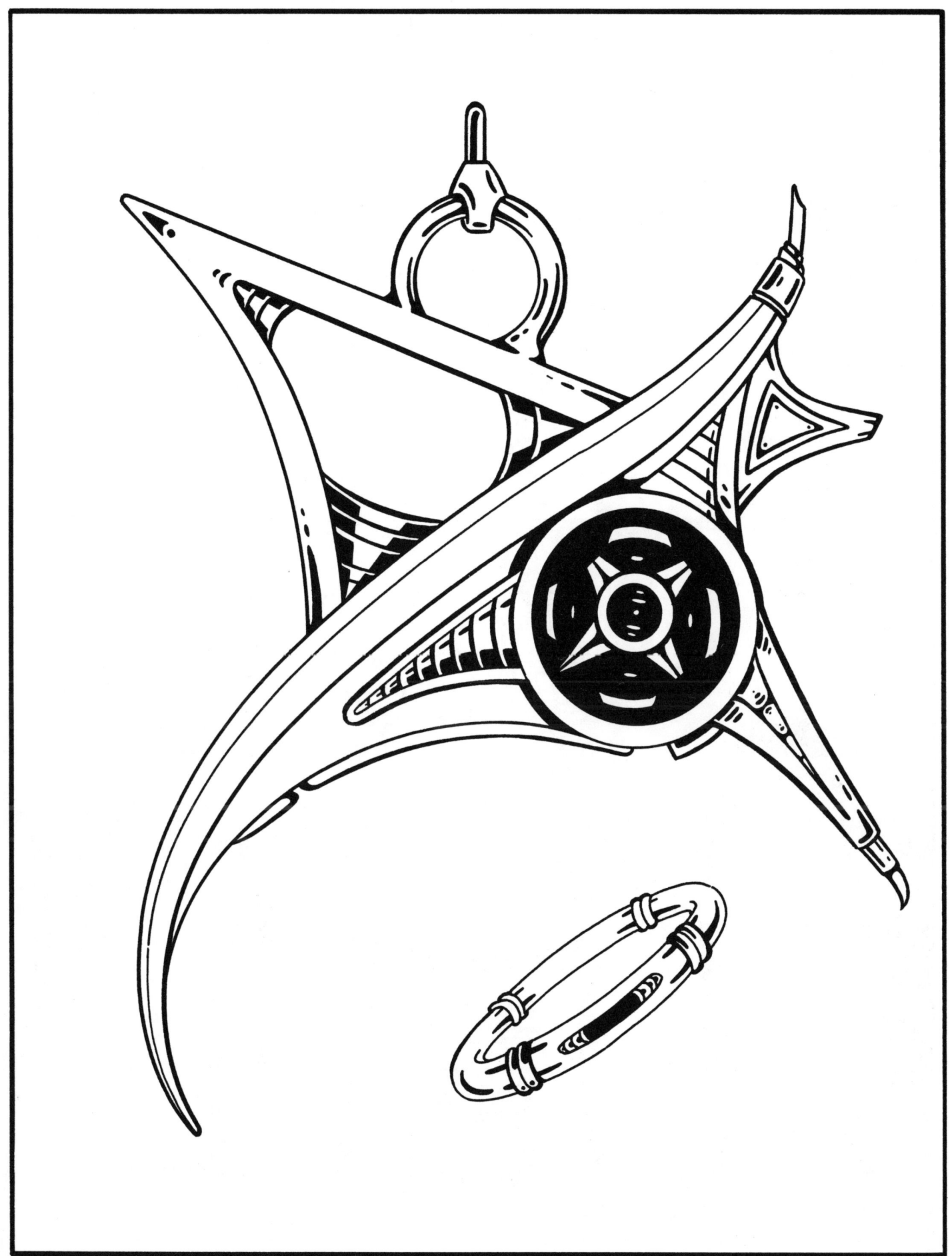

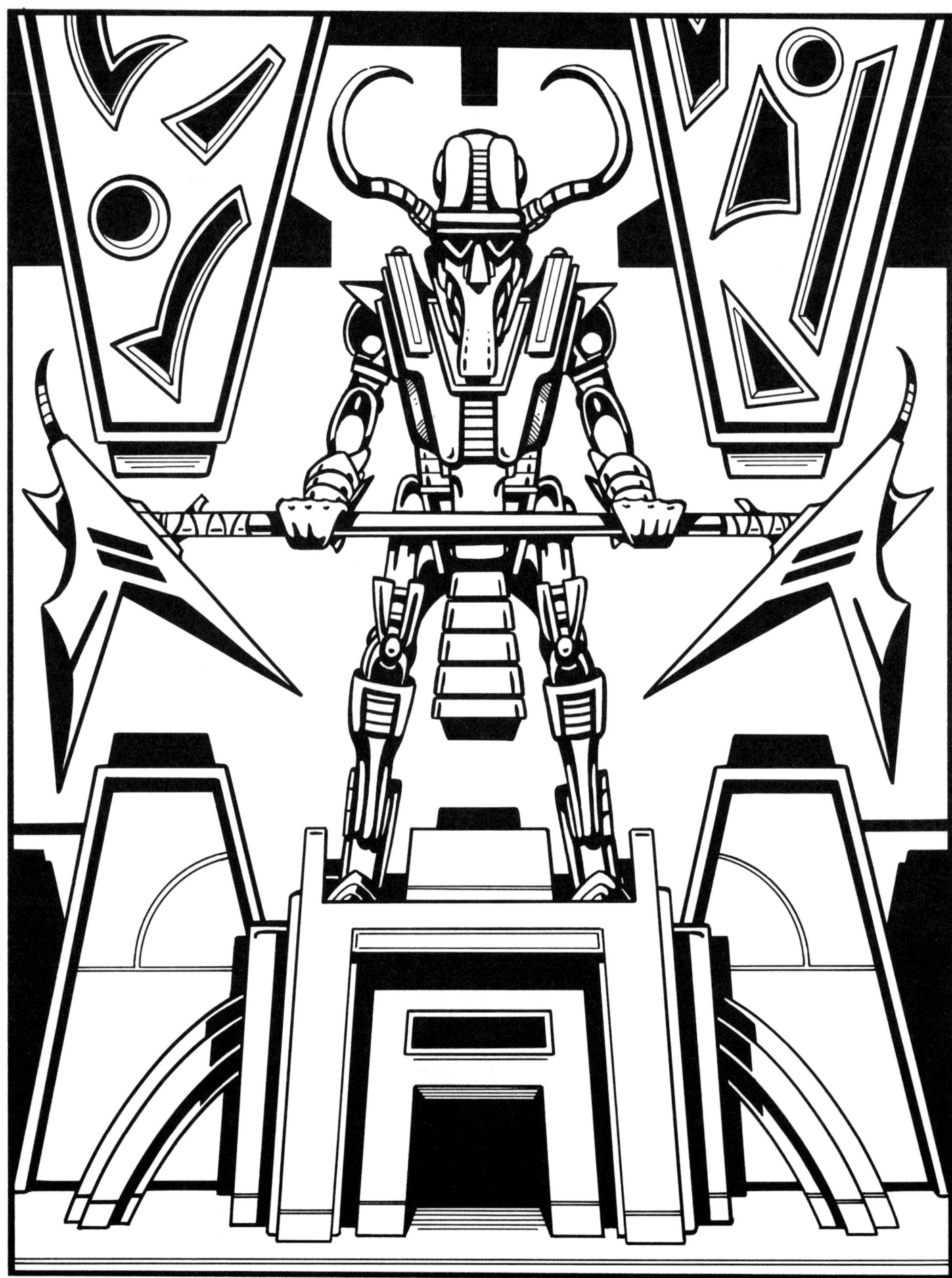

Plate 38

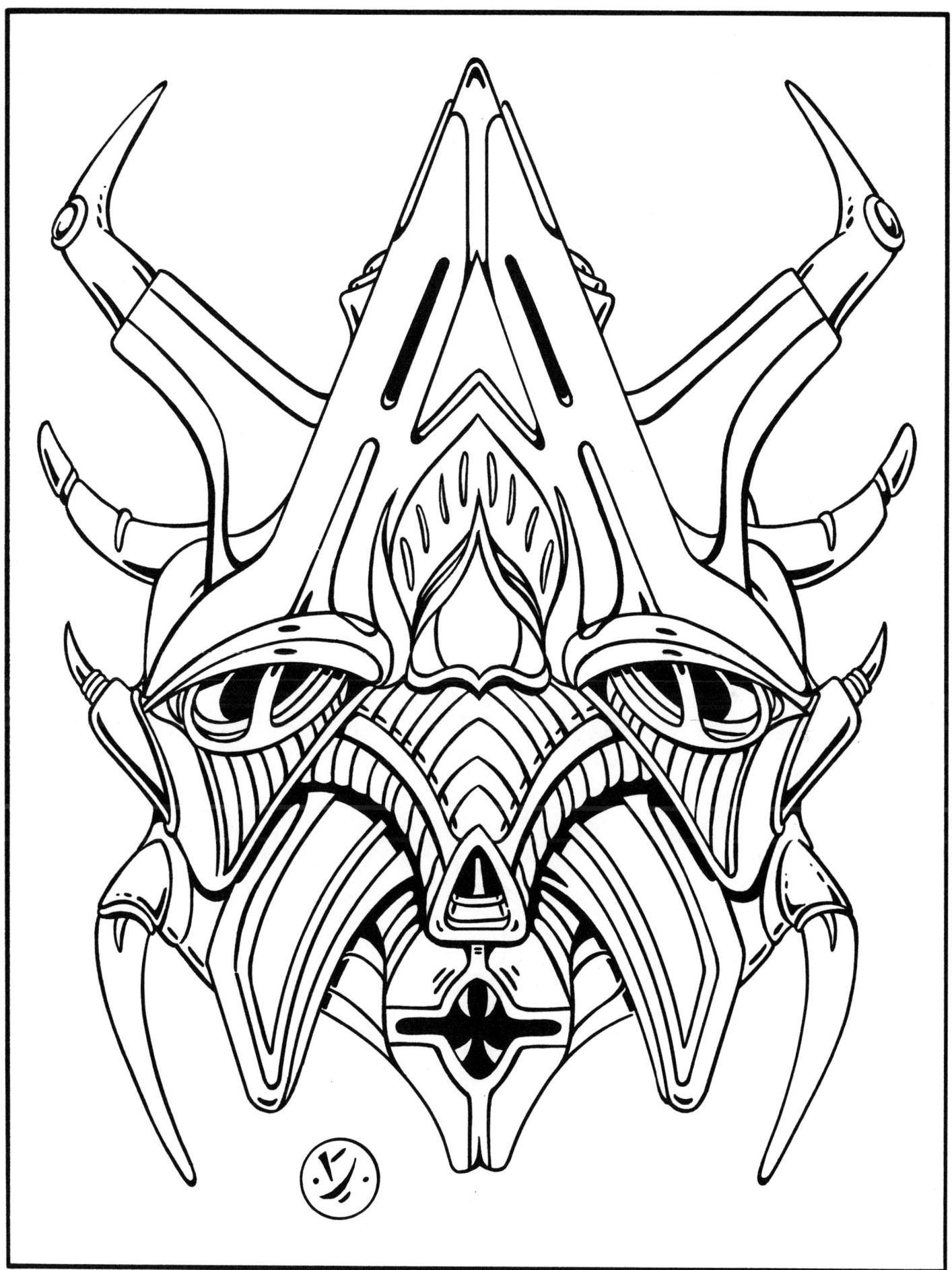

Plate 41

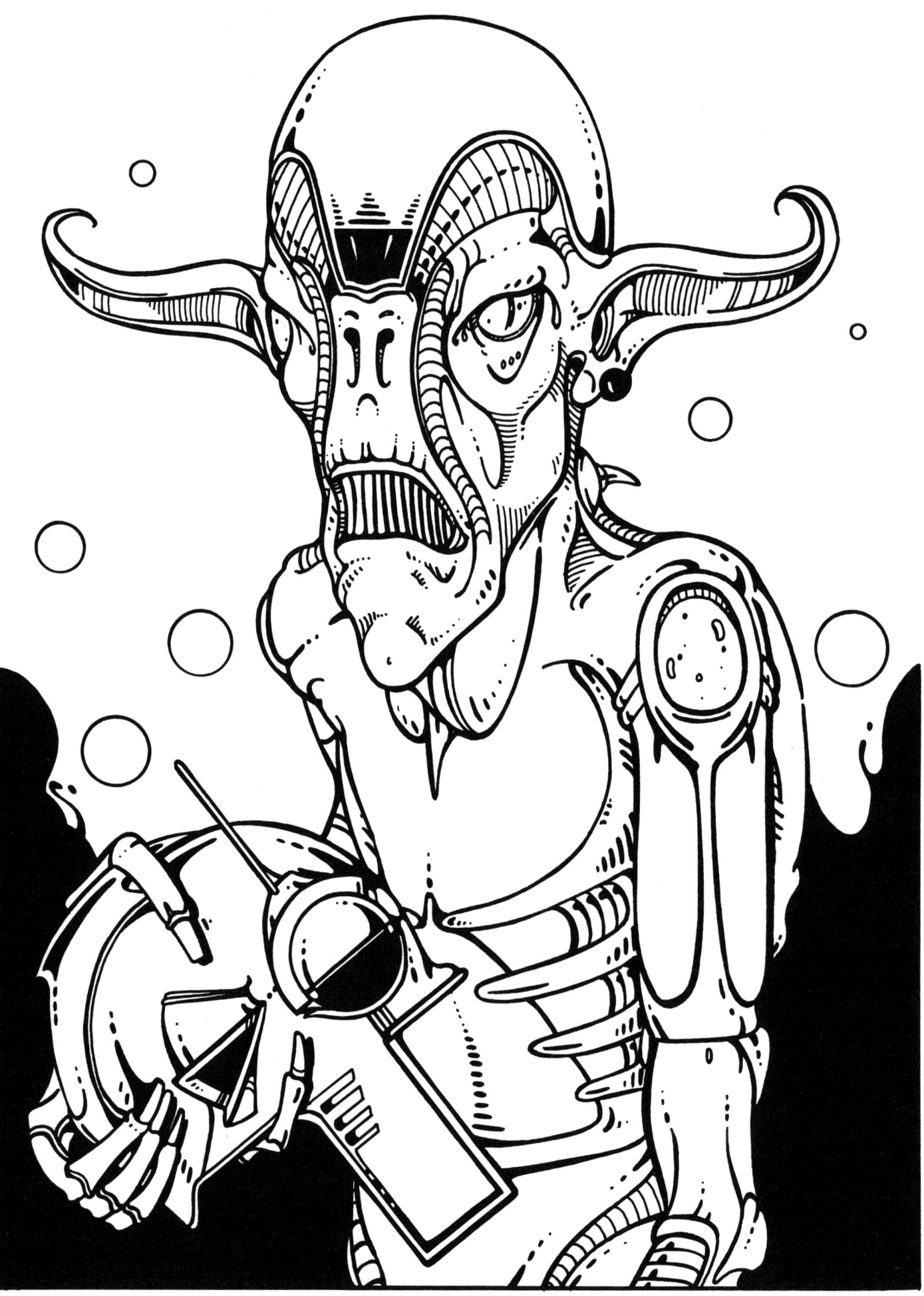